I0692569

Roundell Palmer Selborne

The disendowment of the Irish Church

A speech delivered in the House of Commons, 1869

Roundell Palmer Selborne

The disendowment of the Irish Church
A speech delivered in the House of Commons, 1869

ISBN/EAN: 9783337125752

Printed in Europe, USA, Canada, Australia, Japan

Cover: Foto ©Lupo / pixelio.de

More available books at **www.hansebooks.com**

THE DISENDOWMENT OF THE IRISH CHURCH.

A SPEECH

DELIVERED IN THE HOUSE OF COMMONS,

ON

MONDAY, MARCH 22, 1869,

BY

SIR ROUNDELL PALMER,

M.P. FOR RICHMOND.

ON THE SECOND READING OF

THE IRISH CHURCH BILL.

London:

MACMILLAN AND CO.

1869.

LONDON :
R. CLAY, SONS, AND TAYLOR, PRINTERS,
BREAD STREET HILL.

A SPEECH,

&c.

Mr. Speaker :—

I do not think it is possible that there can be any member of this House to whom this measure has been the occasion of greater anxiety and solicitude than it has been to myself. Almost all the motives which most powerfully actuate and influence human nature would lead me to be desirous of giving my support to the Bill proposed by my right hon. friend at the head of the Government. If general agreement of political opinion were sufficient for that purpose, I may say that there is no man whom for many years past I have so much wished to see occupying the position which my right hon. friend now fills ; and having for nearly nine years been acting in close and cordial co-operation with the party who occupy the benches on this side of the House, I am bound to say that nothing has occurred during that time which has made me otherwise than proud of and satisfied with that connexion, and full of sympathy for the high and patriotic aims which I know to actuate that party in general, and full of personal respect for all the members of it with whom I have been brought into immediate contact. If personal attachments, if a sense of the highest personal and political obligations could be enough to

B

determine any man's course upon this occasion, there are no attachments of mine stronger than those which I bear to some of my friends sitting on the bench below me; and from the first time that I became connected with them until now nothing has been omitted which could possibly have been done to make me more and more deeply indebted to them for every sort of consideration and kindness.

The House will therefore believe that if I am unable to go with them upon this question, it is only under a sense of imperious and overwhelming necessity. My difficulty is not diminished because there are points on which I certainly cannot profess to differ from the advocates of this measure. I have no sympathy whatever with those who impugn the motives either of my right hon. friend at the head of the Government, or of any of those associated with him in this undertaking. I know their motives to be as pure, I know them to be as completely reconcilable in their minds with a just regard to the interests of religion as my own, or as those of any other man ; and I hope that in expressing, as I mean to do with freedom, my own opinions upon this subject, I shall not be betrayed into a single word which can for a moment cast the slightest reflection upon their intentions or motives. Furthermore, I cannot shut my eyes to the fact, that there is a real crisis in Ireland ; a crisis to my mind the more grave and the more serious for the very reason that Ireland has been improving for many years in its condition, for the very reason that the Legislature of this country has shown so much anxious care to make the union with Ireland a real and hearty union. These circumstances, instead of producing a political reconciliation between the majority of the people of Ireland

and the people of this country, seem only to make things worse, and I cannot but think we are called upon, more than at any previous period, deeply to consider the causes of this evil, and discover, if we can, a remedy for those causes. I agree with what was so eloquently said by the President of the Board of Trade, that we ought, if we can, discovering that remedy, to lay aside all party considerations whatever, and be willing to make any sacrifice—be it merely a sacrifice of interest, of prejudice, of feeling, not of duty—which would meet so grievous a state of things ; and even upon the point of the disestablishment of the Church, I shall presently show that there is a certain length to which I might be able myself to go in company with my right hon. friend.

When I look at this Bill, I cannot conceal from myself that the principle of it is not disestablishment simply in the sense in which I use that term, but disestablishment accompanied by universal disendowment. That is a principle to which I cannot agree. It is advocated as an act of justice. To my mind it is a great act of injustice. It is advocated as likely to have salutary and beneficial consequences. I confess that I apprehend from it consequences which may tend to destroy the salutary effect of those parts of the measure, from which I might otherwise have anticipated good results.

It is my duty to inform the House how far I am able to go with the Government on this point of disestablishment. I mean by disestablishment the severance of direct political relations between the institutions of the Church and the laws and government of the State. Taking it in that sense, and carefully separating the question of disendowment from disestablishment, I must say I cannot agree with those who say that the severance of the political relations of the Church with the State is, and necessarily must be, an abnegation of national Christianity, or an act of national apostasy.

It appears to me that such a view is founded on an entirely false notion of the vocation of civil government and of the nature of national religion. The duty of civil government is to govern all and every part of the country committed to its charge with impartiality and justice, and with a regard to those interests which it belongs to human laws to protect. National religion, as I understand it, is not any profession, embodied in laws, or forms and ceremonies, made by those who are at the head of the Government; but it is the religion of the people who constitute the nation. It may be, and must naturally be under many states of circumstances, that the religious convictions of the people will express themselves in the forms and institutions of their Government. Under all circumstances, they must exercise a great influence over public legislation; and, if the rulers are religious men, whether as members of a legislative body like this House, or as administering public authority in any other way, they will carry with them their religion, and be controlled or guided by its moral influence, in the discharge of all parts of their duty. But the forms of national institutions do and must, in this as in all other respects, vary from time to time, according to the circumstances of the country; and it is impossible to lay down à priori a rule to decide whether this change or that change tends to a departure from the national religion. Every single individual will be in point of religion what he was before the change, and therefore, unless you believe that those who advocate the change have themselves departed from the principles of their religious profession, it is a monstrous and self-calumniating thing to say that an act of the nature now under consideration is an act of national apostasy.

These views receive confirmation when they are examined by the light of history. In reality nothing has more changed and fluctuated in form and almost in substance than this idea of Establishment, as applied to the Church in this country, and to the institutions of the State in relation to the Church. The idea of Establishment at this day is different from what it was in the time of Elizabeth and Mary, and down to the time of the Revolution in 1688. It then meant that the Church and its doctrines were by the law of this country incorporated with the laws of the realm, and every person was presumed and commanded by law to be a member of that Church ; and he was punished by the temporal law if he did not discharge the duties belonging to a member of the Church. That is a totally different sort of Establishment from any now existing in this country. There were, doubtless, persons who, when the toleration laws were first introduced, thought that we were giving up national Christianity because we did not any longer compel every citizen to profess the faith of the Church, which had been until then identified with the State. Do we not know, with respect to the penal laws, which all of us now condemn, that there were men who looked on every one of them as a badge and mark of national Christianity, and fancied that if we removed them we should shake the foundations of the faith ? Do we forget how our metropolis was agitated in the last century, when propositions were made for the mitigation of those penal laws, and how it was said that if those propositions should be successful the light of Protestantism would be extinguished. It is well known that many persons declared, when the Roman Catholics were first admitted to political power, that the extension of that privilege to them amounted to a giving up of national Christianity. The same thing was said when we admitted the Jews to this House. But have we been (I speak of the nation as a whole) less Protestant or less Christian since? Those who are Roman Catholics now (still speaking generally) were Roman Catholics then; those who are Jews now were Jews then; the religion of the people is the same, not having in any way altered. These adjustments of institutions to the necessities of civil government, as time went on, simply tended to make the Government a more true and faithful representative of the social condition and actual state of the people; and the exclusion of any classes of persons from their fair share of political power, on the ground that they do not belong to a dominant Church, is no longer recognised as being good either for the State or for the Church. Therefore we must approach the question of any political privilege given to the Church, by considering whether the privilege is for the public good; for if it be not, I am sure it is not likely to be for the good of religion; and, if it were good for religion, it would doubtless be for the public advantage.

In the case of Ireland, I ask myself whether there are or are not valid reasons of State for the existence of that political privilege which constitutes an Establishment, and which may or may not be of utility to the Church. I confess I am at a loss to see in what point of view the political privilege of which I speak is at present useful for the spiritual objects of the Irish Church. We are bound to inquire, first, whether there is or is not reasonable ground for believing that this political privilege of the Protestant Episcopal Church is one of the causes of disaffection among the great body of the Irish people; and, secondly, whether it can be justly maintained for reasons higher and more important than those which are put forward to justify its removal. The hon. member for Hertfordshire, in moving the Address to the Crown on the first day of the session, said that what some people call sentimental grievances are calculated by their nature to excite most substantial irritation. There is real truth in that observation. The same feelings which prompt men to make great sacrifices for political freedom, or for national honour, are excited to resist any form of political ascendency, which is created and maintained by external power in favour of any class, who, if that external power were removed, would have no moral right to claim it. The case is not as if there were one Church Establishment for the whole United Kingdom: Scotland is, for this purpose, separately considered; and it is natural that Ireland should claim to be so too.

But then, if the grievance consists in a violation of the national sentiment, what ought to be the remedy? Why should the remedy go beyond the disease? If the grievance is political ascendency, surely the removal of political ascendency will be the sufficient remedy. The grievance consists in giving, by State Establishment, to the Church of a small minority of the Irish people a superiority of rank, and an exclusive right—a right

which no other religious body in the country possesses
—to have its laws deemed part of the laws of the land,
to have courts maintained for the execution of those
laws—in the association of the Sovereign with the
appointment of its chief officers, like the great officers
of State,—and in the introduction of those chief officers
into the highest seats in one of the two Houses of the
Legislature. These are the signs and marks of political
ascendency, these are the political privileges, these are
the things that cause this rankling and irritation of
feeling; and, in my humble judgment, the exigency of
the case, this so-called sentimental grievance, may be
met by the corresponding remedy—by the removal
of those distinctions which elevate factitiously the
political position of this particular Church above the
other religious bodies in the country. But the question, whether you will take away their property, seems
to me an entirely different thing.

I come, then, to that question; and I ask whether, if
you concede what I have conceded—if you do what I
have stated myself willing to acquiesce in—although,
of course, it would be with reluctance that, belonging
to the Church of England, so long associated with the
Church of Ireland, I could see anything like an appa-
rent diminution of the honour and dignity of the
Church, to which I am deeply attached—yet, conceding
what I have conceded, I ask, is it really a necessary
consequence of it, that you are to introduce and pass
this measure of universal disendowment? I will try
and limit myself to the use of the word "disendowment." It means the same thing with another word,
"confiscation," which I have been quoted in this
debate as using elsewhere, but which I did not use as a
word of contumely. As I take it, that word properly

means taking property not at present rightfully in the coffers or treasury of the State, and putting it there. It is not to be denied that there are occasions and causes which might justify acts properly described by the word "confiscation." The question is whether this is such a case. I confess I think not.

I turn, then, to the question, is this universal disendowment a necessary consequence of taking away political ascendency and political privilege? As a fact, it may possibly now have become so; but if so, who made it necessary? I don't think that such a necessity would be inherent in the nature of the change. I cannot be persuaded that it is a necessity arising from the justice of the case. It may have now become a political necessity; but I can take no part in the responsibility unless I think it always was so, and is also just. I will first ask whether any kind of precedent can be found for it. I confess I know of none. It appears to me unparalleled even by the extensive appropriations of Church property at the time of the Reformation in this country, appropriations which, I suppose, no one will deny, were attended or followed by very serious evils, and which few people have entirely sympathized with, though they may be thought to have been politically necessary. These appropriations were of property belonging to institutions which it was deliberately thought should cease, not merely as then established, but should altogether cease to exist — institutions which were thought practical evils in themselves, and which it was considered the interest, if not the duty, of the State altogether to suppress. Had that been the view taken of the present Church of Ireland, of course we might have admitted the parallel, although we might not agree with the opinion. But every line of this Bill—which from the point of view in which it has been conceived displays the most anxious desire to do as much justice as possible consistently with that view —every line bears witness to the fact, that it is not thought that the Protestant Episcopal Church in Ireland ought to be suppressed, or can or will cease to exist. We have therefore no parallel, even in the extensive appropriations of Church property which occurred in this country at the time of the Reformation; nor am I aware of any parallel cases in any other country, although in some other countries these appropriations have taken place under circumstances so revolutionary as to form no precedents at all. Has anything like this happened in Canada? In Canada, as was well pointed out by the hon. and learned member for the University of Dublin, in that remarkable speech, to which we all listened with so much satisfaction on Friday night—in Canada the whole case was essentially different. There were certain lands reserved by Act of Parliament which were originally supposed to belong to the Protestant Episcopal Church, and it was afterwards determined by law that, according to the true construction of the Act of Parliament, they belonged equally to all Protestant denominations. A large part of these lands had never become profitable : the income arising from other parts, which had never been assigned or appropriated as endowments to any particular rectories or parishes, had been distributed among the Episcopal clergy. These, when the reserves were resumed by the State, were dealt with very much in the way proposed by this Bill—that is, all persons who had got the benefit of the distribution previously made of the income had their life interests respected ; they were commuted ; and, as this portion of the reserves had not been appropriated for the use of any local communities, so as to give them any vested interests in their continuance, there was nothing else to take care of. But there was a third class of lands which had been actually appropriated to the endowment of particular rectories—I think between thirty and forty, or more, as was stated on Friday evening. These lands were appropriated to particular rectories of the Church of England, exactly in the manner in which tithes and glebe-lands are now appropriated to the purposes of the Irish Church. What was done with them ? Were they taken away ? No. They were respected ; they were left. It was felt there was no way of compensating those vested interests, except by leaving the Churchmen of those parishes in the possession of the property ; and they are in possession of it to this day.

But what happened in the United States of America? Surely, if there ever was a case in which this principle of universal disendowment might have been naturally expected to be applied, it was in the case of the separation of the United States from the mother country. In some of the colonies something like ascendency had been given to the Church of England. In the great state of New York there were royal grants—not very old, the latest not much more than 150 years from the time I am now speaking ; very valuable land in the city of New York had been granted for the endowment of Trinity Episcopal Church. We know, on that great Revolution, the great Republic did not think it its Christian duty to establish any particular Church or religious denomination—it was not, I apprehend, less religious on that account—it is only evidence that there was in that great country a divided state of religion which made it inconsistent with civil harmony to introduce such an institution. But did they on that account think it necessary to confiscate and take away the endowments granted to particular Protestant Episcopal Churches, though granted by the Kings and the State of England in previous times ? They did not. It happened, not very recently, that a question arose before one of the Courts of the United States as to the endowment to which I have referred. According to one account which I have received, the value of that endowment is now about 400,000*l.* a year—not so very far from the total value of the endowments of the Irish Church. (A voice from the Treasury bench, " $400,000.") No, the sum was reduced from dollars to pounds in the statement I have received. In another statement, however, the value was given at 100,000*l.*, but, by the falling in of leases, it was thought likely soon to reach or exceed the larger sum I have named. The question was raised, whether Trinity Church was entitled by the laws of the United States to the benefit of that endowment ; or was it to be dealt with as national property, disposable by the nation ? It was held that no law to take it away had been passed by the United States, and till such a law had been passed it could not be so treated. Till you make such a law it is not national property, or to be treated as national property. But what is the key-note of this whole debate ? Why, that this is national property now ; not that we are now to make it so, but that we are to take it as being already so, to treat it as already in our pockets as a reason for putting it there.

I would ask the House further, is there nothing in

the nature of public endowments in any of our own colonies and foreign possessions where there is no Established Church? There are such endowments, as all who are acquainted with the colonies know. I am not sure how it is in India, but certainly in several of our colonies there are such endowments, although no Established Church. The questions of disendowment and of disestablishment, therefore, are not inseparable, and they ought not to be so treated. Whatever other reason can be given for so treating them, it is not a case of necessity. Granting that, I will now ask whether, although it is not necessary, it is right? Upon that question I think that the burden of proof —and much more proof than I have yet heard addressed to that part of the question—lies upon those who assert it. However, I will do my best to accept that burden myself, and I will inquire whether there is any reason for believing that it is just or unjust, that it is likely to be salutary or otherwise; and here, if the House will permit me, I will distinguish a little between the different portions of the revenues of the Irish Church.

I must not be understood as saying that the question of disestablishment might not, to some extent, involve some change in the appropriation of the revenues of the Church. I have never said that, because it is manifest that there may be revenues so obviously connected with the position of dignitaries in an Established Church, as such, that I would not for a moment say, if it ceased to be an Established Church, the *raison d'être* of those particular possessions might not, either to some extent or altogether, cease. That is undeniably the case with the Episcopal revenues, and no one dealing with the question with that degree

of honesty and candour with which I shall at all events
try to deal with it—for I shall express my real opinions
as they appear to my own mind—I say that no one so
dealing with the question can fairly and truly say that
the amount of the Episcopal revenues, or the number
of Episcopal sees, now existing in Ireland, has nothing
to do with the position of the Church as an Establishment. No one can truly say that they have not so
much to do with it, as to make it very difficult here
to separate the question of establishment from that of
endowment. These Bishops are all directly nominated
by the Crown, and they sit by turns in the House of
Lords. Take away the Crown nomination and patron-
age, and the Parliamentary position—let the Church
be reduced to the position of a disestablished Church,
with the right to make and multiply its own offices
and appointments freely, *pari passu* with the other
voluntary Churches of the kingdom—and I cannot
carry the argument myself so far as to maintain
that the same amount of Episcopal revenues can be
claimed by the Church, or that the Episcopal revenues
stand on the same footing as the parochial revenues.
And I will not enter into the question whether or
not it would be just or obviously necessary to take
away the whole of those Episcopal revenues. I wish to
make my argument as cogent as I can on those points
where it seems to me to be impregnable ; and I will for
the moment assume that the burden of proof is so
shifted on myself, as to this point, that I am unable
to satisfy it as to the whole amount of those revenues.
I will also suppose the same as to the capitular
revenues, and also that those funds which are in the
hands of the Ecclesiastical Commissioners are to be
dealt with as in the same category. Those altogether

amount to a very considerable sum, because the aggregate of the three is not less than 186,651*l.* 12*s.* 8*d.* a year. But this leaves untouched the case of the parochial endowments, which correspond with the rectories of Canada and the United States, of which I have spoken, and in which the people have the real vested interest.

Their case stands thus :—The total amount of the endowments of the parochial clergy in Ireland is 395,180*l.* 17*s.* 10*d.*, of which 329,087*l.* 17*s.* 10*d.* is derived from the tithe-rent charge ; the sum of 62,124*l.* 12*s.* 1*d.* from glebes ; and the rest from miscellaneous sources, of smaller amount. How stand the facts as regards the population of the parishes that are so endowed? I find from the Commissioners' report, that, if you take the figures at which they propose to suppress benefices—namely, forty Church members—I do not say whether that is a right principle or not—there are 199 such benefices, with a total annual value of 37,097*l.* 12*s.* 6*d.* In their last appendix they give the total number of parishes having less than 200 Church members, which number is 431. The House will recollect that the total number of parishes in Ireland is something above 1,500. Therefore less than one-third of the whole number are parishes with less than 200 Church members, which includes the 199 parishes having less than forty Church members. The income of these 431 parishes is 54,620*l.* Suppose, then, you were even to take all that away, in addition to the total Episcopal capitular and Commissioners' fund, you would still leave the sum of 340,000*l.* as the present endowment of parishes, in every one of which there are more than 200 members of the Church.

Now, let us consider the sources of these endowments.

It would be a great mistake to imagine that the present Irish Church remains in possession of the whole of the ancient national endowment of the ancient Church of Ireland. The whole course of centuries, down to the present time, has been occupied in its spoliation. Take one item—the tithe-rent charge. That is computed to represent not more than one-sixth of the original value of the tithe. It has been melted away by various processes. A large portion has been appropriated from time to time by lay hands, In the latter part of the last century, when, by several actions at law, the right of the Church to agistment tithe had been established —that is, tithe on pastoral land, and Ireland is a great pastoral country — an Act of Parliament was passed which abolished that tithe altogether. Then we come to the Composition Act of 1823. The compositions for tithes were very much below their value, and by that Act those compositions were made permanent. Then came the Cess Act of 1834, which threw all the repairs which would be met in England by the Church-rate upon the funds of the Church. Then we come to the Commutation Act of 1838, which, as the House knows, gave one-fourth of the commutation, which was paid on the amount of composition, to the landlord as the price of collection. In that way, I find it stated in the second appendix to the report of the Irish Church Commissioners, that the whole value of the remaining tithe is not more than one-sixth of the original value, or, as Mr. Shirley says in his " Historical Sketch," which the Commissioners have published, only a fraction of the original tenth remains to the clergy— scarcely a larger portion than would have fallen to their lot if the whole tithe had been a national provision, and had been divided between the Church of Rome in

Ireland, the members of the other Churches, and the Protestant Episcopal Church itself. Recent measures as to tithes, church-rates, and ministers' money are stated to have had the effect of diminishing the revenues of the Church, even during the present century, by nearly 250,000*l.*, or about one-third of the whole amount. Let us not speak, therefore, as if the entire ancient ecclesiastical revenues of Ireland remain, and are still enjoyed by a small minority of the population. It will be seen, on the contrary, that they are in possession of property not much, if at all, more than equal to their due proportion of the population in general. I do not pretend to put this matter before the House with numerical exactness. I merely mean to say that the disproportion is not anything like what it would be if all or the greater part of the ancient provision made for the Church in Ireland when the people were united in religion still remained in the hands of this small minority.

Now I want to consider what the effect of this Bill would be on these endowments. Practically, the Bill takes away everything, saving only the life interests, and private endowments since 1660. I will consider the life interests presently ; but I want now to know whether there is really and truly a clear and satisfactory distinction between these private and non-private endowments. I know that my right hon. friend the member for South Lancashire—I ought to have spoken of my right hon. friend by that title, which I am much more happy to apply to him —that of Prime Minister of England,—I know that my right hon. friend is perfectly aware that, except as a matter of sentiment, there is no distinction, because he said so. In his speech at Liverpool he said that the sentiment was irresistible. I confess I agree with him. I think the sentiment is irresistible, when you propose to take away private endowments. But I carry it somewhat further. 1 think it is equally irresistible with regard to all parochial endowments whatever. I have said there is no distinction in principle between the case of private and other endowments. And why? Because the private endowments were given to the Established Church. And if it be true that the glebes given by kings—and the tithe given by ancient piety, and afterwards consolidated by law—are to be regarded as given to the Church only as an Establishment—given on condition of the continuance of its privileges by the State, as a Church having its institutions united by law to the political institutions of the State—it is irresistible logic that the donors of these private endowments must be held to have given them just as much to the same Institution, and for the same reason. The real truth is, that if you try to find any solution of the question, you must look to general considerations of reason, policy, and justice; and I say that reason, policy, and justice oblige the man who takes away to show the reason why he does it. To my mind that reason has not yet been shown.

But now let us consider what this distinction between public and private endowments, since the Reformation, really is worth. The whole of the glebes in Ulster, and by far the greater part of those in other parts of Ireland, were given after the Reformation. And how were these estates given? Were they given by Acts of Parliament or by solemn acts of the State, to which you can refer, and on the face of which you can find that the gift was upon condition of the continuance of the existing state of relations between the institutions of the Church and the institutions of the State? They were given by kings, out of lands which came by confiscation into the hands of those sovereigns, exactly as those sovereigns gave other portions of the same lands to private persons, whose descendants enjoy them to this day. I own it was a matter of some surprise to me to hear, I think from my right hon. friend, but, at all events, from one speaker on the Treasury bench, that these glebes, and parts of the tithes which are dealt with by the present Bill, were given by way of restitution, because they had previously been taken from the Church by some former process of disendowment. It certainly is a very formidable doctrine that you are to go back from the existing title to a more remote title, which had been destroyed, and, on the ground that the new title is to be referred to the old, to conclude, for some reason connected with the old, that the property itself is to be taken away. A most formidable doctrine this, I must say, and especially for the new voluntary Church body, which you are going to create under this Bill. According to that doctrine, there will certainly be no security for the new Church body—no security for the churches or houses which may be left to them—no security for anything which may be saved through the commutation of their life interests. For these may all be said to be, in some sense, a *residuum* remaining out of the old endowments. I confess it seems to me, that when a State gives freely and does not annex specified conditions—when Kings, more especially at periods of our history which enabled them to deal with property as if it were altogether their own, or when private individuals, give property to persons capable of taking it by legal titles, titles as valid at the time of the gift or grant as any private titles could be—when that is done, the gift takes effect exactly in the same manner, to all intents and purposes, whether the donor be the King, the Parliament, or a private individual. You must look at the title, see when it was granted, and what conditions were annexed, and if the conditions were the same in one case as in the other, there is no more justice in taking away the property in the one case than in the other.

I have thus given my reason for not thinking, that you can possibly stop at private endowments, or at Churches, if you recognise the principle of some moral claim on the part of this body, even after it should cease to be established. I may, perhaps, be permitted to say one thing more in this connexion. If we are to frame for ourselves hypotheses as to the motives and reasons for these grants, and to say it was because the Church was established, and it was supposed it would continue to be established, that these gifts were made, and that now it is to be disestablished these grants are to be withdrawn and to revert to the country, I should like to know, that line of argument once adopted, where we are to stop? I pointed out in the early part of these observations that the Established Church did not mean the same thing at all periods of our history, that it was very different before the Toleration Acts from what it was afterwards. Before the Toleration Acts, the idea was, that the State and the Church were absolutely one, and everybody was bound by law to be a member of the Church. Some one may improve upon the view I am at present combating, and may say, that the reason why all the endowments granted to the Church, at all events from public sources, down to the Revolution of 1688, were so granted, was because at that time all persons were supposed to be of one religion, and were, in fact, required to be so by law; but that the law on that subject being changed, *cessante ratione cessat lex.* In other words, such a line of argument puts it in the power of any one taking a retrospective view of history to annex conditions, not expressed, to all ecclesiastical property whatsoever, and, because of the changes which have occurred in our legal, social, and political systems, to say that those unexpressed conditions have been violated, and therefore that the State has the right to resume the property. That, I say, would be a new and very formidable doctrine.

Then I come to the next point, the limit of 1660. The principle upon which that date has been adopted appears to me more difficult to understand, than almost anything else in the Bill. It is said, that, because the Thirty-nine Articles of the Church of England were not adopted by the Irish Church until 1634—not 1660—and because the system of Church government and Church discipline in Ireland may have been practically consolidated, in its present exact form, after the Restoration rather than before, you are therefore to take matters as if an entirely new start had then been made, and a new Church established, and as if all kinds of endowments given between the Reformation and that date of 1660 had been given to some Church other than the present. But those who say so cannot possibly be ignorant of this plain matter of fact, that by the legislation—which few of us entirely approve—of the 2d of Elizabeth, it was expressly stated that the whole of the bishoprics in Ireland were to be in the nomination of the Crown, as they were in England, and even more absolutely; that the Liturgy of the Church of England, as such, was to be in use in all churches in Ireland, and everybody was to be obliged to conform to it; and that this included the Ordination Service, and everything else characteristic of the constitution and discipline of the Church of England. And although it may be true that the Thirty-nine Articles were not adopted till 1634, will anybody say that there was not substantial community of doctrine and of worship in the two Churches in the interval—at all events as far as the law was concerned; or will anybody say that persons who gave private endowments during that interval gave them with a view to the Roman Catholics usurping the benefices, as they did in some portions of the country during a considerable part of that interval, or with a view to Episcopalian clergymen fraternizing in other places with Presbyterians,—as my right hon. friend said they did fraternize—possibly very much to the benefit of both? It is evident that the gifts must have been to the Church then established by law, and not to some other Church which, as the law stood, could not then exist. The suggestion is, that there was a good deal of confusion, and a good deal of usurpation of benefices in different parts of Ireland, by persons not conforming to the Established Church, during the interval of which I have been speaking. I believe that there is much exaggeration in this statement; but if it were ever so true, it could not justify the assumption that persons who gave endowments to the Church established by law before the year 1660 did not mean the same thing as persons who gave endowments after that date. Why, the very confusion, the very invasion by Roman Catholics here, and Presbyterians there, must have made the induce-

ment stronger to give new endowments to the Church
to replace what she had lost.

And now I come to a question of much more importance. Why do you respect only life interests?
Are there no others? I say there are. And the Bill,
in this respect, seems to me the *ne plus ultra* of that
system,—I hardly know how to characterise it without
using some word stronger than I should wish to do—
of that practice which too much prevails in our legislation, of looking to the individual interests of persons
who discharge public duties, more than the rights and
interests of those for whose sake they discharge them.
It is a distinguishing feature of the present working
system of the Church of England, that there is hardly
anything for which a clergyman once appointed can
be turned out of his living. But who are the persons
who have the real interest and benefit in the ministrations of the clergyman? The people of that religion
whose minister he is. They are the persons whose
servant he is. And when you find that there is a
community, necessarily permanent, which your legislation neither will destroy, nor is meant to destroy,
who will continue after it has taken effect with the
same spiritual needs as before, and obliged either to
go with these needs unsupplied, or to find new pecu-
niary means for their supply, then, I say, the true
vested interest is the interest of those persons, and
not that of the minister.

Now, let us look at what is proposed. It is proposed to give to these persons their churches—a costly
boon. Let me not for a moment be misunderstood.
I should be truly sorry if they were not to have their
churches. But still it is a costly boon. We find from
the Commissioners' report that at this moment the

total annual cost of their maintenance, including repairs, for the year 1867, was 62,043*l*. 17*s*. 11*d*. They have been maintained out of the Church funds exclusively—not a shilling, not a penny has been levied from the people, since the abolition of cess in 1834. You are now going to throw that 62,043*l*. 17*s*. 11*d*. upon the members of the Church, besides everything else, although they will no longer have the Church funds to assist them. Now, let us see how the fact stands, as to whether there are such persons—large permanent bodies, in parishes as populous as ordinary English parishes are—who have the local claim, who will continue to have it, and from whom you are taking away this property, not to give it to anybody else; for this disposal of the surplus—although I have not a word to say against it if there be a surplus—is manifestly an ingenious discovery under great difficulties, for the purpose of finding out what to do with it.

Now, let us see whether there are in truth such people as I have referred to, existing to any great extent in Ireland. I find it stated in one document appended to the Commissioners' report, that, in one-third of the dioceses in Ireland, all the parishes are sufficiently populous to require the exclusive services of a resident ministry, so that it would be inexpedient and unfit to unite any other parish to them ; and that, as to the other two-thirds of the dioceses, one-half of the parishes are so. That is the general statement; but it applies still more forcibly to particular parts of the country. With the permission of the House, I will take for illustration two dioceses in the north of Ireland—first, the united diocese of Derry and Raphoe, and, secondly, the united diocese of Down, Connor, and Dromore.

In the first of these dioceses there are 111 benefices, to only 20 of which is there attached a less church population than 200. One of them has more than 3,000, 17 of them between 1,000 and 2,000, 3 between 900 and 1,000, 7 between 800 and 900, 9 between 700 and 800, 7 between 600 and 700, 14 between 500 and 600, 12 between 400 and 500, 11 between 300 and 400, and 10 between 200 and 300. Now, anywhere else, should we say that these were not cases in which the population was adequate to a permanent endowment? I say nothing against anybody who might suggest, that by possibility in some of those places the endowment may be excessive, and more than can be justified by the population. If such be the case, let that be the subject of investigation and adjustment. I would yield this, as I have yielded some other things for the sake of peace, where I was not bound by justice to maintain them. But surely these are populations, which have some right to say, " We ought not to suffer. You are taking away from us our permanent endowments, although you provide for our servant the minister, and are giving us in return no compensation whatever, although we want an endowment as much as ever we have done, and have not done anything whatever to forfeit it."

Let me now take the population connected with the benefices in the diocese of Down, Connor, and Dromore. Of 11 parishes in Belfast the aggregate population is 24,534. Of the remaining 133 parishes only 24 have a population under 200 ; 1 has a population of above 5,000, 1 between 4,000 and 5,000, 6 between 3,000 and 4,000, 9 between 2,000 and 3,000, 17 between 1,000 and 2,000, 7 between 900 and 1,000, 3 between 800 and 900, 8 between 700 and 800, 7 between 600 and 700, 11 between 500 and 600, 7 between 400 and 500, 15 between 300 and 400, and 17 between 200 and 300. From these 109 parishes, having such a substantial population, you propose to take away all provision for a religious ministry.

But this does not apply only or principally to populous parishes in towns, where it is comparatively easy to supply the religious wants of the population. The Rev. Mr. Sadler, a clergyman of the Church of England, who has written a very able pamphlet upon this subject, and in whose views I may say I almost if not altogether agree, has given a table of the Protestant Episcopal population in 44 parishes, merely as examples, and many more might be found. He has excluded from that table all places containing either the whole of any large towns or any parts of them. In every one of those 44 parishes there is a population of at least 300, and in many of them much more, and they are scattered over no less than 25 square miles, and in some instances over 35 square miles, being eight times the area of average English parishes. In one of those parishes there is a population of above 4,000, in another of above 3,000, in two of 2,000, in thirteen of 1,000, and so on below that number. In those cases the people are in such circumstances, that it is very difficult indeed to suppose, that if you take away from them the existing provision for religious ministry they will be able to supply one for themselves. But is it not quite plain, that, unless you can show that in taking away that provision there is some manifest good to be done—that it is to be given to somebody who has a better right to it—you are doing a wrong to these people? Because I say that, to take away my property, not because it belongs to somebody else, but because you want to take it away, is doing me a wrong.

Passing from that point, I would ask, what would be the result of the change you propose to effect? And here I will take the liberty to refer to the appeal which was so eloquently made by the right hon. gentleman the President of the Board of Trade on Friday last, in that splendid speech, which we all heard with so much interest. May I be excused if I respectfully take the liberty of saying, that I listened to that speech, and all other recent speeches made in this House both this year and last, by the right hon. gentleman upon this subject, not merely with intellectual admiration, but with a very large degree of moral sympathy. He does not accept my conclusions ; he thinks both them and my reasoning entirely wrong ; but I do take the liberty of saying, that with the feeling which actuated and animated him in those speeches I entirely sympathise ; and it is only because I think that unjust which seems to him just, because I think that although his end is good his means are not so, that I do not go along with him, as, if I were merely to indulge my feelings after hearing his powerful appeals, I might be disposed to do. The right hon. gentleman endeavoured to show that, after all, the effect of the proposed change would not be the spiritual destitution of these communities of the Church. I wish to avoid the fallacy of generalising, by speaking of the Church as a whole. I will, therefore, not speak of the Church as a corporation, because hon. members have been very properly pulled up for speaking of the Church as such. When you speak of the Church as a whole, you lose sight of some of the main points of the question. It is of the endowed communities, of the people

in the parishes, that I want to speak. The right
hon. gentleman says, "Why entertain such gloomy
views? Why have you not more faith in the power
of your religion? Don't you remember what happened in Scotland? Don't you remember that magnificent spectacle?"—and it was a magnificent
spectacle, one of the finest moral spectacles which
history has ever presented—"of that great body of
men who went out for conscience sake from the
Establishment, without any compensation for vested
interests, leaving house and home, and immediately
betaking themselves to the founding of a new
Church,"—with that remarkable and extraordinary
result, which the right hon. gentleman so powerfully
depicted.

I would, however, ask the House whether there is
not a very great fallacy in pointing to that spectacle
as an example to us at the present moment, as if that
case possibly could be like the one we are now
considering?

In the first place, I beg to observe, that the State
has dealt very differently with the Established Church
in Scotland from the way in which she has dealt with
the Episcopal Church both in England and in Ireland.
The Established Church in Scotland enjoys, in my
humble opinion, a much better government, a much
better organization—I don't allude to the difference
between Presbytery and Episcopacy, of course—than
the Church of England. She has her Kirk Sessions,
her Presbyteries, her Synods, her General Assemblies,
each step of self-government rising above the other,
so that she has been well exercised in the whole art
and power of self-government, self-legislation, and
self-expansion, no State control coming in to stop her

synods from meeting, or from exercising all necessary powers of legislation and discipline. There the great men who afterwards became the leaders of the Free Church movement had as much liberty of speech as we have in this place. There they formed their parties, there they organized their system, there they collected together such a power and bond of moral public opinion as enabled them to go forth triumphantly, even when leaving all which in this world they possessed.

Have you so dealt with the Church of Ireland? Have you not imposed upon her, as the very condition of the Establishment which you now seek to remove, such restraints as prevented that organization of the powers of self-government, that organization of ways and means, and that organization of feeling, opinion, and discipline, which we have seen existed in Scotland? I am not speaking of an abstract difference, I am speaking of a difference which had a direct practical bearing upon the very case itself; because how was the Free Church formed? Was it the birth of a moment? Did it spring up full armed like Minerva from the head of Jupiter? By no means. It was formed in the General Assemblies of the Established Church. There it was that, by legislation, by council, by deliberation, by carrying on a long battle against the powers of the State, the principles of the Free Church were established and consolidated, and the bond of union formed between those who afterwards seceded. But has anything of the kind occurred, or could anything of the kind have occurred, in Ireland? If it had, you might have said, "The Irish Church has disestablished itself, and must take the consequences."

The next observation I have to make is this,—There

is all the moral difference in the world between the man who goes out of his own accord and the man who is turned out. The man who goes out of his own accord goes out in a cause in which he is the aggressor at all events, and may think he will be the conqueror; but the man who tries to hold his own, and is not able to do so, is in a very different situation, and a very long period indeed must elapse before he can arrive at the possession of an organization suitable to his altered condition. Mr. Bence Jones well remarks, that a " a man reduced from wealth to poverty is in a very different state from one who has never been otherwise than poor, and has numberless difficulties of which the other knows nothing."

Now, as to the Voluntary system. Certainly I am not one of those who have ever stood up to abuse the voluntary principle. It has done great things, and may do great things again. Christianity conquered the world under the voluntary principle; and, no doubt, in the times in which we live, it looks a little as if the world was endeavouring to reconquer Christianity, under the opposite arrangement. But though endowments may not be the *summum bonum* which some persons seem to believe them to be, we have, I think, a right to consider, whether those who have lived under endowments can be able all at once to do equally well without them. It is said, that if the Church in Ireland should be disendowed the Protestants will be able to provide for themselves. In proof of that proposition, it is said, that the Roman Catholic Church in Ireland is able to provide for herself now by the voluntary principle. The Roman Catholic Church in Ireland does so, but certainly by means in which the clergy of the Protestant Church of that country are not instructed—by means to which the people of the Established Church are not accustomed. A Church in possession of large endowments is able to give a gratuitous ministry. Such a Church makes its people accustomed to a gratuitous ministry ; but of course, a Church which is organized on an opposite principle accustoms its people, as far as their means go, and sometimes above their means, to contribute to their own spiritual wants. Undoubtedly, in the course of time, the Church which is now endowed in Ireland might accustom itself to the voluntary system ; but how long a time will be necessary for that purpose ? How long a period will be required to teach those who have always relied upon a gratuitous ministry to do otherwise ? It appears to me, that independently of all the changes which it may be found necessary to make in its system of local organization, you must take a long time before you can arrive at that.

I think there is a fallacy in the argument used by those who say, that the rich in Ireland belong to the Church with which we are dealing, and that the poor chiefly constitute the Roman Catholic Church in that country. It does not quite follow that because the rich belong to a Church they will contribute to it with a liberality proportionate to their means, especially if, as in this case, many of them are not residing on their properties ; nor does it follow, that, if they do not do so, the poor will not be the sufferers. Who will be the sufferers if a ministry be not provided ? Will it be the rich non-residents, or even chiefly the rich residents? No. It will be the poor, the permanent local poor—they will suffer most. You don't suppose they will change their religion upon account of the passing of this Bill. If they are not in circumstances to pay their clergy,

are the clergy to depend on the rich ? Bishop O'Brien
says :—

"To the successful working of the Voluntary system numbers
are of much more importance than wealth, and the diffusion of
the wealth of the religious community than its amount."

And he quotes Isaac Taylor, who observes :—

"No motive that has hitherto been brought to bear upon
human nature has availed to make the rich liberal after the
proportion of the poor."

But I would not have it supposed that in this case
I am willing to do injustice to the rich. I ask
the House to consider their position. They will for
forty-five years, at all events, continue to pay tithes,
though they will not have provided for them that, to
provide which, and which only, tithes exist. It is
true that their titles do not comprehend that interest
in the land ; but it is also true, that the tithe rent-
charge never was State property in any sense whatever.
Tithe rent-charge, since the law established it, (and the
law only established it because conscience had done so
before,) has only existed as a charge on land for the
express purpose of providing religious ministrations.
It may be said that some of it has been appropriated
by lay impropriators. That was done in bad times,
and I don't think that such an arrangement could
now be repeated ; but I say this, that tithe rent-charge
is a local charge, that it never was imposed and never
could have been imposed for general or Imperial purposes, and it would be most unjust to use it for such
purposes. I have high authority for that. I have
a speech which contains these words :—

"Those funds, gentlemen, are local funds. The tithe of a
parish was never given except for the purpose of maintaining

religion in the parish; and to take the tithe out of a parish of Galway or Clare for the purpose of meeting the wants of Protestant congregations in Dublin or Belfast, whatever the intention may be, is — I care not who hears it — in my opinion very like indeed, and dangerously like—whatever the intention may be, that is quite another matter—an act of public plunder."

Whose words are those? They are the words, spoken during the last election, at Newton, of my right hon. friend at the head of the Government. I don't for a moment suppose there is a syllable in them from which my right hon. friend would now shrink. I have no doubt my right hon. friend would repeat those words now; but if those funds are local funds, if the tithe of a parish was never given except for the purpose of maintaining religion in the parish, and if to take the tithe out of a parish in the west or the south of Ireland for the purpose of maintaining religion in the north or the east is very like an act of public plunder, I own that I think the transfer must have the same complexion, if you withdraw such a local fund from a parish in one part of the country for the purpose of maintaining in another part of the country—no one knows where—for the purpose of maintaining lunatic asylums. I don't understand that the lunatic asylum need be in every particular parish. I don't understand that there is to be even any approximation to that principle in the scheme of my right hon. friend. The real truth is, that the funds described by my right hon. friend as " local funds," are funds which it is now proposed to treat as ordinary State property, disposable in any manner that Parliament may think useful on the whole, and which it is proposed to transfer from spiritual to secular, from local to general purposes. What I think on this point cannot be better stated than in the words of a very able man, the Knight of Kerry. He says—

" It may be held to be quite right that a great public good should be effected, even where it inflicts wrong on an individual ; but it is fair at least to admit that it is a wrong. I think the case may be made more clear, by excluding the ecclesiastical element for a moment, and treating it on ordinary principles of business. Suppose, for example, that all the estates in this country were liable to a charge of, say 1s. per pound for the maintenance of some necessary local institution—the county hospital, for example —which we will suppose, moreover, had for centuries been supported from this fund and this fund alone ; would not all the landowners of this county have just cause of complaint, if an Act of Parliament seized the above fund for the public exchequer, and left them either to support the hospital out of their own pockets or to allow it to collapse ? I confess it does seem to me that a serious injustice would be done in this case, and I cannot possibly see where the parallel fails."

Hitherto, I have dealt with the sufferings and loss that will be inflicted upon this portion of our fellow-countrymen ; and I will now inquire as to the reason. First of all, have they done anything to forfeit the advantages which they enjoy ? Now, I confess it seems to me, that the considerations applicable to that question, instead of leading to an affirmative conclusion, greatly add to the weight of everything which I have already advanced. How has the State dealt with this Church in past times ? It has loaded her with all the evils, with all the drawbacks, and with all the difficulties, arising from the grossest misgovernment, from the grossest and most profligate spoliations, and from those detestable penal laws which have done so much to alienate from this country the hearts of the people of Ireland. I certainly think that it is much more owing to the acts of the State than to anything that she has done, that the Church has been laid open to the charges which are made against her. And, therefore, I do not think that the State is warranted in regarding as a ground of forfeiture that degree of failure in the Church in Ireland, which is mainly attributable to bad civil Government and bad legislation, more especially as it is admitted on all hands that in our own time she has done her duty well. I may here refer to the expenditure which is proved to have been made upon the faith of these endowments since 1833. We read not only of all the churches and parsonage-houses in Ireland being built since the Reformation, but the total expenditure in building and improvement of churches and parsonage houses amounts to a million of money since 1833, and that is only the expenditure, to the recorded proofs of which the Ecclesiastical Commissioners are able to refer. Now, let us consider for a moment, whether you do justice, when you treat that as the measure of the claim upon you, which such an expenditure creates. You cannot separate private and public expenditure in such a matter as this. You must take into account all that has been done on the faith of the possession of these endowments. Those who have supplied this money may fairly claim to have considered, not only the money which they have actually laid out, but all the other circumstances which attended that outlay. If I contribute 100l., and the Ecclesiastical Commissioners give 50l. in aid, is it to be said that I am not entitled, as a purchaser, to the aggregate endowment ? Some talk as if the wrongs done in former times ought now to be visited, by way of retribution, upon the Irish Church of this day. But if the people who now derive benefit from those endowments are wholly innocent of those wrongs, if their clergy have been, far beyond the memory of the present living generation, exemplary, useful, and efficient, and have given no ground for complaint, it is impossible to make out a cause of forfeiture against those communities, which the moral sense of those communities at all events can be expected to recognise and allow.

I will not weary the House by referring in detail to other considerations, connected with the immigration into Ulster, with the plantation of Ulster when the improvement of lands, formerly waste and wild, was undertaken by a Protestant population, invited to come there upon the faith of their possessing an endowed Church. They were promised, and they received, a Church endowment of so many acres, in a fixed proportion to the number of acres improved and brought into cultivation by them. This part of the case is powerfully and clearly set forth in a recent declaration, numerously signed by Protestant gentlemen in Ireland ; and, as it has probably been read by most members of this House, I do not feel myself justified in repeating it here.

I will now endeavour to grapple with the argument so often adduced, and which is really the main assumption on which all the other arguments in favour of this measure are founded, that this is public State national property, which is at the present time misappropriated for the benefit of a few, when it belongs to all. That appears to me to be a doctrine which is, not on technical grounds of law, but upon substantial grounds of law and fact, absolutely untrue, in the sense in which it is brought forward. I do not mean for a single moment to deny, that the nation has a large interest in and control over every species of

public property. But of public property there are
various kinds. There is that in the public exchequer,
contributed by the taxes of the country, and there is
that which is vested in the nation at large, or in the
sovereign, for purposes co-extensive with the general
government of the country. These are national property, in the largest and fullest sense of the word.
But every species of property, given for every kind of
use beneficial to any portion of the community—the
property of municipal corporations throughout the
kingdom, the property of the City companies, the property of the Universities and of the colleges in the
Universities, the property of all hospitals and charities
—is in a certain sense public property, subject to public
regulation and control; and in the due management
of this species of property the public has always an
interest. But that is a sense, in which every one
would perceive that the State would not be warranted
in treating it as disposable at its own mere will and
pleasure. And, on the other hand, the public interest in
it is not of that nature, which would warrant any one
in saying that the State can be called to account for its
use and application, as if the State were annually giving
the same amount of money for the purpose out of the
public exchequer. There is a confusion of thought,
when we fail to perceive that there are many grada-
tions of what, to some extent, may be regarded as
public property; and that money belonging to a portion of the community ought not to be taken away by
the whole of the community, unless good cause of
forfeiture or proof of misuse can be clearly made
out.

Now, it seems to me that to apply this principle to
the local parochial endowments, in which the local

communities have an interest, to deprive them of that which they would either have to supply out of their own pockets, or, still worse, go without—is much more unjust, than if you were to apply it to any kind of corporation which would cease to exist upon your taking away its means. Take the case of the monasteries, for example. They absolutely ceased to exist when they were by law dissolved ; you dissolved communities which then, in the nature of things, necessarily came to an end as soon as the individual members, who were then living, died. So it would be in the case of the colleges at Oxford and Cambridge. There is no permanent body of persons which would continue after their dissolution, and be a loser. The public, or the Church, might be a loser, by the destruction of valuable institutions ; but there would be no individual persons who would be in want of what they, or their predecessors, had before. But here you are dealing with a permanent class of persons in the enjoyment of local funds, who will remain and continue in existence after you have done this, who will want those funds afterwards as much as they did before, and who will either have to supply the deficiency themselves, or go without that which is much more valuable. I cannot but think, therefore, that this plea of national property is altogether unsound.

Now, I frequently hear the word "prescription" employed by hon. gentlemen opposite. Prescription signifies a title established by enjoyment for a length of time, where there is no proof of any original right. But in this case we have, with enjoyment for a great length of time, a clear legal title to that enjoyment. How did the House think it right to deal some years ago with the case of the charitable trusts in this kingdom which were enjoyed by Unitarians, but were originally founded for the benefit of Trinitarian congregations? The congregations had gradually lapsed into a different faith, and for much more than twenty years Unitarian congregations had been in the practical enjoyment of funds to which the courts of law determined they had no legal right. My right hon. friend, and Lord Macaulay, and other great authorities, said it was right even to legislate in that case for the purpose of applying the principle of prescription. I am wholly at a loss to understand why the claims of congregations of our own faith in Ireland, whose legal title is so much better, and who can urge the enjoyment of centuries in their support, should not be at least as much respected; or why the rights of those persons who have from time to time laid out their money, and made all their arrangements on the faith of the continuance of these endowments, should not be equally regarded. And certainly it is not an answer to say that the legislation of 200 or 300 years ago, which settled the existing title to a portion of these endowments, was a violent and oppressive legislation. Because wrong was done then, you cannot take from those who have had a valid legal title for centuries that which they have done nothing to forfeit, simply on the ground that at a remote period your predecessors may have done something equally unjustifiable.

Another great argument which I will take the liberty of referring to is the argument of equality. That seems to me, in the sense in which it is put, to be a very dangerous argument. It is new to me, that it is the business of the State to abolish all inequalities of property. Of course nobody contends for this as affecting individuals ; and nobody, in truth, contends for such a principle, as that it is the business of the State to abolish inequality of property among religious bodies, whether they have or have not been originally created by means of public endowments. As far as I have heard in these debates, and in recent discussions of these subjects by advocates of the present measure, everybody repudiates the application of such a principle to Scotland or England. This principle of equality, when it is brought forward to justify you in taking away local funds from those who have done nothing to forfeit them—not to give them to anybody else, not to restore or redistribute them, not to establish another Church because it is the Church of the majority, as in Scotland, but simply for the purpose of taking them away,— appears to me to be a principle which cannot be worked out without going much beyond the point, to which anybody at present is proposing or desires to go. You will be producing another new form and state of inequality, in some respects more remarkable, between one part of the kingdom and the other parts of it. It would be one thing, if you were about to found another Established Church—it would be one thing, if you were only resuming superfluous endowments ; but it is a very different thing, for the sake of bringing about equality between different classes in Ireland, to take away from one religious body, whose title is one of centuries, everything by which its possessions exceed those of another which does not advance any claim to have such possessions for itself. Although we do not carry the principle further, there may be some who will. I look with great suspicion upon a principle which if it is logically pursued, may lead to conclusions which we all repudiate, and which we desire everybody to lay aside, because there is so great a difference, as all agree there is, between the case of the Established Churches of England and Scotland and that of Ireland. Well, then, let us legislate in a manner which that difference suggests; but do not let us lay down an abstract principle of levelling equality, as a reason for doing what on other grounds we do not justify.

I have thought it my duty to say what I felt upon this subject. I do most heartily desire and pray that all my apprehensions may be disappointed; I do heartily desire that all those good effects may follow which my right hon. friend desires, and I am sure expects, from this measure. I have said nothing upon the subject of danger to private property, because it appears to me, that there is in the nature of things a broad and clear line between private property and all property of this character. At the same time, I am bound to acknowledge, that the circumstances of the present times are peculiar, especially in Ireland; and that in Ireland language has been and is held as to private property, which in a manner connects it with some of the same considerations, which points to its origin from confiscations in past times, and which parades the fact that it is for the most part held in Protestant hands—language which, I think, does in some measure justify the alarm of those who fear danger; and, however well we may mean, if, while proceeding in one direction we make a false step, if we go too far, if we go beyond the limits of justice in dealing with this description of ecclesiastical property, we may be helping, perhaps not to kindle, yet to fan the flame, which threatens also property of other descriptions.

I trust that my right hon. friend may deal successfully with what is called the Land question. From what was said the other day by the right hon. President of the Board of Trade, we know it is not intended to deal with it in a manner which can in the smallest degree do violence to or infringe the principles of the security of property. Whether or not all the desires and hopes which have been excited in Ireland on that subject will or can be satisfied by any measure fulfilling that condition, remains to be seen. I most heartily hope and trust that they may; but of one thing I feel confident, and it is, that we should be safer and upon surer ground, if we were not to permit ourselves to be led to hope we can be doing good, by violating the just rights and reasonable feelings of our Protestant fellow-subjects. Are they not people who have deserved well of the Crown? Whatever in their position has been false or unfortunate, has been much more owing to our legislation than to themselves. If that position has been made false with a view to fortifying English interests in Ireland, I cannot but think it would be a very unjust and ungenerous thing if we were to treat them as if they had deserved ill rather than well of us for their share in fortifying those interests. They have been loyal, intelligent, and industrious subjects of the Crown, and if they are not numerically the most important, they are a very important class of her Majesty's Irish subjects. Surely, in doing that which is needful to allay discontent, and to sow the seeds of a better feeling among other parts of the community, we should be very cautious how we wound their feelings, disregard their interests, and alienate them, perhaps, without really conciliating other classes, who are now discontented.

I repeat, I heartily wish and pray that the expectations

of my right hon. friend of good from this measure may
be fulfilled. I do not say they may not. Although I
have offered the best arguments I could command, I am
by no means insensible to the force—in many cases the
great force—of the arguments urged on the other side.
I have told the House how far I can, and how far I
cannot go. It only remains for me to say, that if this
House shall pass, as I presume it will pass, in substance, this measure, I shall, for one, acquiesce in the
verdict of the House and of the country; and I will do
my best in committee to suggest improvements in
those details which, as it seems to me, are capable of
improvement, of course without attempting anything
which may be inconsistent with the decision of the
House. I trust and hope that, if this measure should
pass into law, the members of the future disestablished
Church of Ireland will not take the advice which
seemed to be offered to them from the benches opposite a few nights ago,—will not think they are asked
to co-operate in their own destruction, by having put
into their hands the means of organization for future
activity and usefulness, and, as I trust, of future
revival and prosperity. I hope they will gird themselves up like men, and will use the means offered
them—and, putting details aside, I know no better in
the main than those suggested — of completing the
reconstruction of their Church upon the Voluntary
principle; and although it cannot be without a sense
of great and grievous wrong and injustice, yet still
I hope they will submit, like men and patriotic
citizens, to a wrong done to them by those who sin-
cerely believe it for the general welfare, and will contribute as far as they can to that end, by setting,
notwithstanding all they may have suffered, as good

and bright an example of loyalty to the Crown as they have set before, and at the same time bury in oblivion all feeling of irritation, all feeling of animosity towards any other classes of the community, and endeavour to bring about, even out of this measure, so injurious to them as I cannot but think it is, as much as possible of future good.

THE END.

LONDON: R. CLAY, SONS, AND TAYLOR, PRINTERS.